# Picture This!

guide to choosing books for young children

Published by Clare County Library
© Clare County Library 2002

This publication has been grant-aided by the National Reading Initiative

ISBN: 0 9541870 0 8

Books selection and reviews by Patricia Fitzgerald.

Design and Layout by Jackie Dermody-O'Brien.

Printed by Colour Books, Dublin

Clare County Library,
Library Headquarters,
Mill Road, Ennis, Co. Clare.

# Introduction

It is the policy of Clare County Library to actively promote the reading habit, not being content to simply stack books on shelves, and hope that our readers will find them for themselves. Our overall aim is to increase access to material. The main focus on adult fiction promotion to date has been to make people aware of the rich variety of literature available from many countries and traditions. Commencing in 1993 with "Voices from Europe", a collection of contemporary novels in translation which explored aspects of life on the continent, formal book promotions continued regularly.

The enthusiasm of Patricia Fitzgerald, Senior Library Assistant, Children's Services, ensured that children and young adults were not forgotten in this development. A "Children's Book Award Winners" promotion was followed by "Irish Authors for Children". Teenagers were enthralled by their own Book Promotion "Books with Attitude", "Thrillers and Spinechillers" and "Kiss and Tell". These promotions are featured on the library's website at www.clarelibrary.ie

This current joint venture with the National Reading Initiative entitled "Picture This!", is the brainchild of Patricia Fitzgerald and she has put in a tremendous effort to ensure quality and balance in her selection.

I am sure all parents will agree that the titles selected and described provide a treasure that will instil a love of books and reading. We hope that the stories chosen will help illustrate the ordinary everyday experiences of childhood through a combination of words and pictures in a way that will appeal to parents and children alike.

I would like to thank Patricia for her drive and energy in bringing this aspect of the promotion to fruition. I would also like to thank children's author Siobhán Parkinson for writing a foreword to the collection.

I would also like to thank Jackie Dermody-O'Brien, Senior Library Assistant, who has brought her creative I.T. skills to this project. This marriage of the traditional book and new technology shows the way forward. Information Technology helps to promote reading and the work done by Patricia is brought to a worldwide audience by the skills of Jackie and the use of the library website.

*Noel Crowley,*
County Librarian.

## Foreword

One of the very greatest pleasures of parenthood – and grandparenthood, godparenthood, uncle-/aunthood – is reading picture books to and with small children. In fact it brings such joy, to both adult and child, that I am tempted from time to time to borrow the occasional child expressly for this purpose.

Reading with small children is never just about reading words. It is about sharing the story, looking at the pictures, anticipating favourite moments, repeating well-loved pieces of text, finding new things in the illustrations. These are all great sources of pleasure in themselves, and they are also valuable skills that will help children when they come to learn to read.

In fact, reading picture books has a lot to teach adults about the nature of story. Accustomed as we are to reading 'grownup books', we are inclined to focus on text, and to think that stories can only be told in words. Small children can rediscover for us the joy of 'reading' the pictures along with the words.

Children who have grown up on picture books have an endless source of pleasure that they can draw on all their lives. No child is ever 'too big' for picture books. If you think about the pleasure you get yourself from reading with young children, you will realise that the joy of picture books can continue way beyond the early years. Returning to picture books that they enjoyed when they were younger and the world was an easier place is a great comfort to a child who is finding the going tough. There are also many, many wonderful picture books that are intended for older readers. In fact, children can continue to enjoy the special pleasure of picture books, alongside their other reading, right into their teenage years and beyond.

In every library and bookshop there is such an array of picture books that it's sometimes difficult to know where to start. That's where a guide like this is so valuable. You can be sure that all the books recommended here are excellent of their type, and the thematic arrangement will help you to find the books that will appeal to your child and suit his or her interests or needs. And finding one book by an author or illustrator that you like is only the start of it. You and your children can then move on to read other books by the same author and from there can venture to new authors and new artists.

Let this book be your guide on a wonderful journey through the picture-book section of your library, and I promise you that you will find books to enchant you and your children for now and for years to come.

*Siobhán Parkinson,*
Author

# Growing Up

## Well Done, Little Bear
### Martin Waddell

This book in the delightful "Little Bear" series is no exception to the quality of picture books written by Martin Waddell. Little Bear goes exploring, with Big Bear close by to offer encouragement. Only when he feels Little Bear needs help does he interfere, saying, "I'll be there when you need me . . . always."

*Ar fáil trí Ghaeilge dár dteideal, Maith thú, a Bhéirin.*

Published by Walker Books Ltd.
ISBN: 0-7445-5590-6
Illustrations © Barbara Firth 1999

Published by Walker Books Ltd.
ISBN: 0-7445-1925-X
Illustrations © Virginia Miller 1991

## On Your Potty!
### Virginia Miller

Parent and child will enjoy this hilarious approach to potty training. Bartholomew's antics are those of any small child who's not quite sure what his potty is for until the end of the story when he is rewarded for his efforts by a great big hug from George.

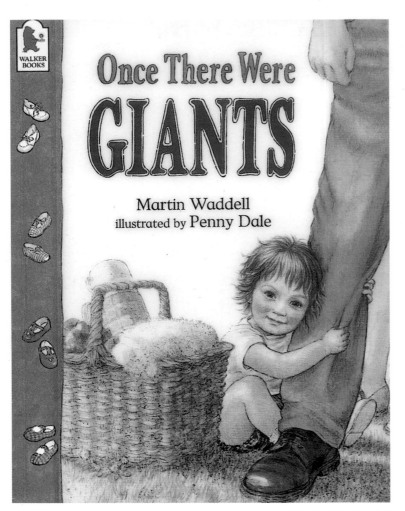

Published by Walker Books Ltd.

ISBN: 0-7445-1791-5

Illustrations © Penny Dale 1989

# Once There Were Giants
## Martin Waddell

A lovely telling of baby's development to adulthood with a touch of humour as well. When the baby was little there were giants in the house. At the end of the story the baby has become one of those giants herself and now has a baby of her own. Young children will ask for this story to be read and reread. Each page depicts a warm family situation with a little hint of mischief too.

*Ar fáil trí Ghaeilge dár dteideal, Bhí Fathaigh Ann Uair.*

# John Joe and the Big Hen
## Martin Waddell

Another picture book treasure from Martin Waddell. John Joe wanders away while left in the care of his big brother Sammy and his sister Mary. He finds himself eventually in the Brennan's yard being confronted by the Big Hen. This is a simple story with characters and references, which are typically Irish. The situation where older children are left to look after a little brother or sister is easy to identify with and will appeal to children up to six or seven and perhaps older.

*Ar fáil trí Ghaeilge dár dteideal Seáinín agus an Chearc Mhór.*

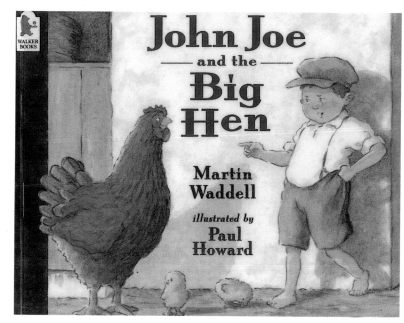

Published by Walker Books Ltd.
ISBN: 0-7445-5243 5
Illustrations © Paul Howard 1995

## Freddie Visits the Doctor
### Nicola Smee

One of the O'Brien Toddlers series. This book will introduce your child to the doctor's waiting room, the doctor and to what the doctor does when you visit, suffering from a sore throat. Freddie is accompanied by Bear who is also showing the same symptoms. Strong card pages with simple bright illustrations will quell any fears your child might have about a visit to the doctor.

Published by The O'Brien Press Ltd.

ISBN: 0-86278-536-7

Illustrations © Nicola Smee 1997

# I Want My Potty

**Tony Ross**

Published by Andersen Press Ltd.
ISBN: 0-86264-137-3
Illustrations © Tony Ross 1986

## I Want My Potty
### Tony Ross

Guaranteed to make all frustrated parents and confused children see a funny side to potty training. A hilarious portrayal of everyday life by Tony Ross. Your toddler will take consolation in the fact that even princesses have accidents.

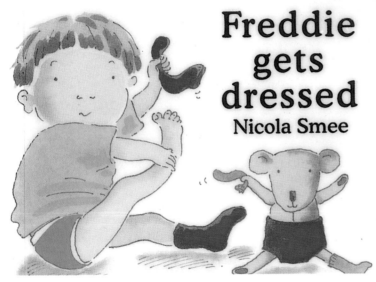

**Freddie gets dressed**

Nicola Smee

Published by The O'Brien Press Ltd.

ISBN: 0-86278-535-9

Illustrations © Nicola Smee 1997

# Freddie Gets Dressed
## Nicola Smee

Another of the O'Brien Toddlers series, this sturdy picture book, suitable for pre-school children provides for discussion on getting dressed, something every small child decides it's time to do alone at a certain stage. Freddy decides to dress himself and bear, often ending up in hilarious situations as he tries to master the art of getting dressed.

# Titch
## Pat Hutchins

The emotions of little Titch in this story are palpable in every page without ever being told to the reader. Small children will know exactly what Titch is feeling with words like "Titch was little. His sister Mary was a bit bigger. And his brother Pete was a lot bigger." The story takes a lovely turn at the end when the three children plant a seed. Pete provides a spade, Mary, a flowerpot, but it's Titch who plants the seed that grows into an enormous plant. Very little text with superbly simple and striking pictures makes this a great read for the youngest in any family.

Published by Red Fox
ISBN: 0-09-926253-3
Illustrations © Pat Hutchins 1971

## Starting School
### Janet and Allan Ahlberg

The first week at school is described in detail with the text on each page interspersed with pictures. Everything a child encounters on the first day at school is explored, from where to hang the coats to going to the bathroom. Funny, sympathetic and realistic, this is an excellent introduction to school for nervous beginners.

Published by Viking
ISBN: 0-670-81688-4
Illustrations © Janet and Allan Ahlberg 1988

# Child Participation

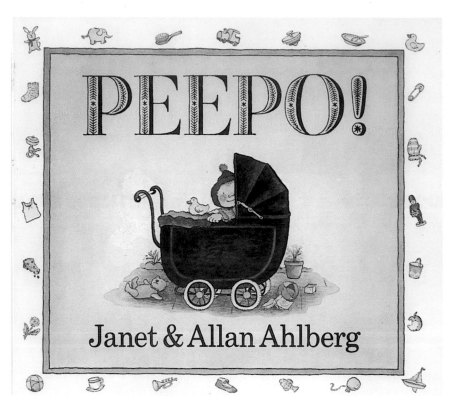

Published by Viking
ISBN: 0-670-80344-8
Illustrations © Janet and Allan Ahlberg 1981

## Peepo!
### Janet & Allan Ahlberg

A classic picture book ideal for sharing. Mothers, fathers, older brothers and sisters will enjoy sharing this book with the little one in the family and discussing what baby sees on each page.

# From Head to Toe
## Eric Carle

Bright drawing in collage
fashion typical of Eric Carle
books encourage your child to
move his body from head to toe
in imitation of the animals on
every page.

Published by Puffin Books
ISBN: 0-140-56378-4
Illustrations © Eric Carle 1997

## Quacky Quack-Quack!
### Ian Whybrow

A fun way of teaching children different animal sounds. This beautifully illustrated picture book with rhyming text and lots of repetition is irresistible for any young child who wants to join in while it's being read.

Published by Walker Books Ltd.

ISBN: 0-7445-3037-7

Illustrations © Russel Ayto 1991

Published by Andersen Press Ltd.
ISBN: 0-86264-830-0
Illustrations © Emma Chichester Clark 1999

# Follow My Leader
## Emma Chichester Clark

A beautiful book for very small children to participate in. The little boy in the story enjoys an exciting game of follow my leader with lots of animal friends until he is faced with a dilemma; should he let the tiger join in? Enjoy the wonderful illustrations and discover how the problem is resolved through pages of fabulous pictures with few words.

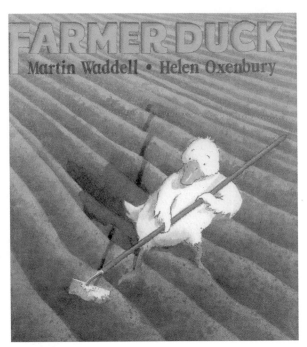

Published by Walker Books Ltd.
ISBN: 0-7445-1928-4
Illustrations © Helen Oxenbury 1991

# Farmer Duck
## Martin Waddell

The name Waddell is synonymous with picture books. Farmer Duck is as much a commentary on social issues as it is a classic picture book for the small child, older siblings and indeed adults. The constant refrain of "how goes the work?" by the lazy farmer provides for repetition and joining in as do the different animal sounds on each page. Just as in Owl Babies, the pictures compliment the text to produce an excellent combination of illustration and story. Published in 1991 it is as much a favourite with children now as it was on publication in the last millennium.

*Ar fáil trí Ghaeilge dár dteideal*
*An Lacha Feirmeora.*

## Cock-a-Doodle-Doo
### Steve Lavis

A bright colourful way
to familiarize your child
with numbers and
animals. Each double
page offers much to be
explored and discussed

Published by Puffin Books
ISBN: 0-140 55942-6
Illustrations © Steve Lavis 1996

## Oink!
### David Wojtowycz

Ideally suited to toddlers, this sturdy board book teaches children animal sounds. Each animal is attached to the book by a colourful ribbon, the exercise being to jumble the animals around and slot them back into the correct page, matching the sounds they make.

Published by David & Charles Children's Books

ISBN: 1-86233-084-0

Illustrations © David Wojtowycz 1999

# LITTLE COPY CUB

Catherine & Laurence Anholt

Published by Hamish Hamilton Ltd.
ISBN: 0-241-13969-4
Illustrations © Catherine Anholt 1999

## Little Copy Cub
### Catherine & Laurence Anholt

Little Cub is someone you will want to hug from the very first picture you see of him on the first page. Children are invited to do like little copy cub as he mimics the antics of Big Golden Lion and the other animals in the jungle. This is an excellent book for reading aloud, for child participation and for learning in the nicest possible way.

Published by The O'Brien Press Ltd.
ISBN: 0-86278-523-5
Illustrations © David Wojtowycz 1997

# Rumble in the Jungle
## Giles Andreae

A colourful parade of wild animals described in noisy rhyming verse. A lovely introduction to animals in the wild.

# Letters and Numbers

# Alfie's Numbers
## Shirley Hughes

Learn to count with Alfie, each page of this delightful book showing scenes from many favourite Alfie stories. Children who have read other Alfie books will be happy to learn to count with familiar characters like Annie Rose, Mrs. McNally, and Alfie's Mum and Dad.

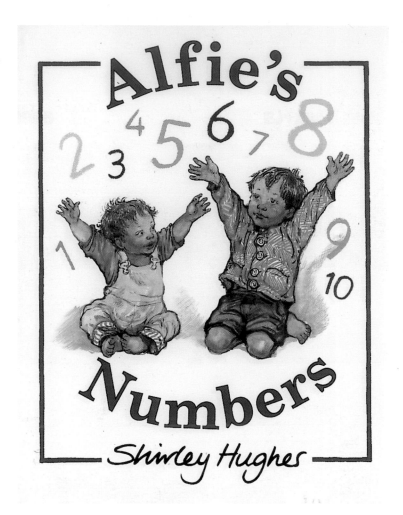

Published by The Bodley Head Children's Books
ISBN: 0-370-32591-5
Illustrations © Shirley Hughes 1999

Published by Walker Books Ltd.

ISBN: 0-7445-6007-1

Illustrations © Flora McDonnell 1997

# Flora McDonnell's ABC
## Flora McDonnell

Big bold drawings on background pages of different colour will appeal to small children and make learning the alphabet much more fun. Small children will be immediately attracted to this book because of its size and colour.

Published by Hamish Hamilton Ltd.
ISBN: 0-241-14075-7
Illustrations © Shirley Hughes 1984, 1987

# Lucy and Tom's 123 and ABC
## Shirley Hughes

Lucy, Tom and their parents are at home today because it's Saturday. We see that numbers and counting are a big part of the day's events. Children learn to count and to appreciate numbers in this storybook without even realizing it. There are plenty of opportunities for discussion within the warm family atmosphere portrayed by the excellent pictures one expects in any book by Shirley Hughes.

# Ten in the Bed
## Penny Dale

"There were ten in the bed and the little one said, Roll over, Roll over!" This is an ideal picture book for child participation based on the traditional nursery rhyme. Warm bedroom scenes on each page, which a small child can explore and talk about, encourage familiarity with numbers.

Published by Walker Books Ltd.
ISBN: 0-7445-1340-5
Illustrations © Penny Dale 1988

# Home and Family

# You and Me, Little Bear
## Martin Waddell

Here is another story by Martin Waddell about Big Bear and Little Bear. Little Bear wants to play but Big Bear is too busy, a familiar situation for small children. Like all the bear stories this one creates a warm loving atmosphere and offers plenty for you and your little child to chat about.

*Ar fáil trí Ghaeilge dár dteideal Mise agus Tusa, a Bhéirín.*

Published by Walker Books Ltd.
ISBN: 0-7445-6721-1
Illustrations © Barbara Firth 1996, 1999

Published by Walker Books Ltd
ISBN: 0-7445-5596-5
Illustrations © Jill Murphy 1993

## A Quiet Night In
### Jill Murphy

It's Mr. Large's birthday and Mrs. Large plans a quiet night in to celebrate. Not surprisingly in the Large household things turn out a bit differently than planned. Mr. & Mrs. Large fall asleep on the couch while the Large children take the food upstairs deciding it's a pity to waste it. An enjoyable funny story with bold bright illustrations.

Published by Walker Books Ltd.
ISBN: 0-7445-6720-3
Illustrations © Barbara Firth 1991, 1999

# Let's Go Home, Little Bear
## Martin Waddell

The familiar characters Big Bear and Little Bear feature again in this attractive picture book. The worries of Little Bear are explained and soothed by Big Bear. Little Bear is frightened by various noises when out for a walk but Big Bear soon puts him at his ease and carries him back home to the comfort of their cave. Just as in Can't You Sleep Little Bear and You and Me Little Bear the illustrations are simply gorgeous.

# A Piece of Cake
## Jill Murphy

Mrs. Large embarks on a healthy living campaign putting the whole family on a diet. Anyone who has been on a diet will identify with the longing for forbidden treats. Mrs. Large creeps out of bed for a slice of cake to discover there's only one piece left and is caught in the act by the rest of the family when she enters the kitchen. She ends up agreeing with Luke who says "I think elephants are meant to be fat". The illustrations are warm, familiar and funny, giving the sense of a real family setting.

Published by Walker Books Ltd.
ISBN: 0-7445-5595-7
Illustrations © Jill Murphy 1989

## So Much
### Trish Cooke

Winner of the Smarties Book Prize in the 0-5 category in 1994. Family life is portrayed at its happiest in this picture book. The story focuses on the love shared by all the relations for the little baby in the family, so much so that one is almost surprised at the end to discover that everyone has called to the house for Dad's birthday party. Bold bright pictures by illustrator Helen Oxenbury show us how everyone wants to squeeze, kiss and love the baby "so much."

Published by Walker Books Ltd.
ISBN: 0-7445-4396-7
Illustrations © Helen Oxenbury 1994

The Large Family
Five Minutes' Peace

Published by Walker Books Ltd.
ISBN: 0-7445-5594-9
Illustrations © Jill Murphy 1986

## Five Minutes' Peace
## Jill Murphy

Mrs. Large escapes to the bathroom for five minutes peace from her three children, or so she thinks. All mothers will empathize with her as each child in turn competes for her attention. Mrs. Large's situation is similar to that of every mother with small children. She has no chance of finding time for herself, not even five minutes.

Friendship and Sharing

## My Best Friend
### Pat Hutchins

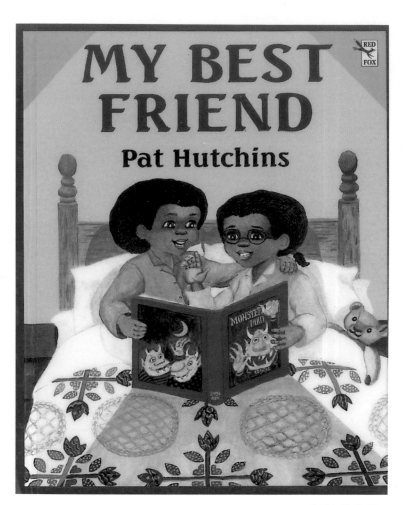

Published by Red Fox
ISBN: 0-09-928191-0
Illustrations © Pat Hutchins 1993

It's wonderful to have a best friend who can eat spaghetti with a fork and not drop any, untie her shoelaces and do up the buttons on her pyjamas. But even the most capable of best friends need help sometimes. The little girl in this story is glad to put her best friend at ease when she thinks there's a monster in the room. That's what being best friends is all about.

## Pumpkin Soup
### Helen Cooper

This is a story about friendship and sharing. Three friends, Cat, Squirrel and Duck do the same things each day, like making pumpkin soup. Everyone has his own job to do, everyone is happy or so it seems. Like all good friends these three argue about who does what and why. After a falling out Duck leaves the little white cabin and gives his friends time to think. They worry that Duck has found nicer friends and is not coming back. Instead Duck returns, all three swap around their chores and order is restored again, at least for the time being. A clever funny story is made all the more interesting by striking pictures and not too many words. One of

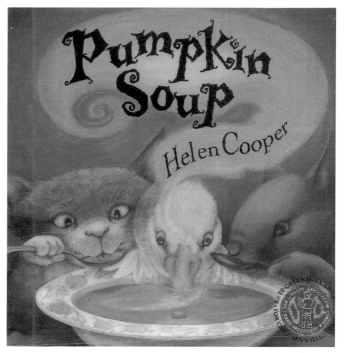

Published by Picture Corgi Books
ISBN. 0-552-545101
Illustrations © Helen Cooper 1998

# What Newt Could Do For Turtle
## Jonathan London

When Turtle pulls Newt from the mud declaring that's what friends are for, Newt wonders what he can do to return the favour. He is even more indebted to Turtle when he saves him from an alligator. But Newt gets a chance to save his friend's life before they settle down for the Winter's sleep. This book is a reminder of the importance of saying thanks and will prompt the young reader to remember similar experiences.

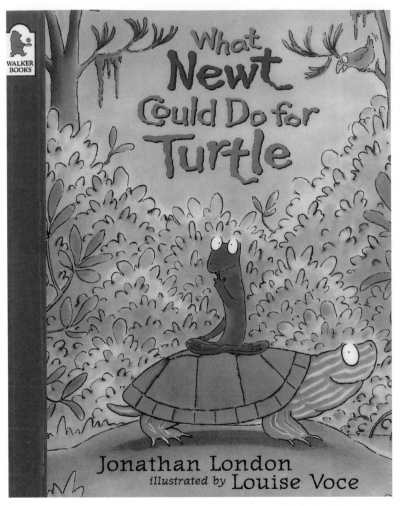

Published by Walker Books Ltd.

ISBN: 0-7445-5493-4

Illustrations © Louise Voce 1996

# Brothers and Sisters

Published by Walker Books Ltd.
ISBN: 0-7445-4489-0
Illustrations © Simon James 1997

## Leon and Bob
### Simon James

Many children have an imaginary friend just like Leon. One day a boy named Bob moves in next door and takes the place of Leon's imaginary friend who incidentally is also named Bob. Cleverly written and beautifully illustrated with line drawings it explores the theme of friendship in a way that is understandable to young children.

## Brand New Baby
### Bob Graham

Edward and Wendy are typical, curious children awaiting the arrival of their baby brother or sister. They are also typical in their reaction to baby Walter when he is born. How life changes not only for Mum and Dad when a new baby arrives but also for the little people in the house is realistically described in this book.

Published by Walker Books Ltd.
ISBN: 0-7445-6141-8
Illustrations © Blackbird Design Pty. Ltd. 1989

# Watch Out!
## Big Bro's Coming
### Jez Alborough

Little Mouse tells all his friends Big Bro's coming and frightens them all into believing he is huge and awesome. A funny surprise ending will make children laugh and realise how silly the animals and maybe even the children themselves have been. Beautiful big pictures of animals in the jungle are an added attraction.

Published by Walker Books Ltd.

ISBN: 0-7445-6304-6

Illustrations © Jez Alborough 1997

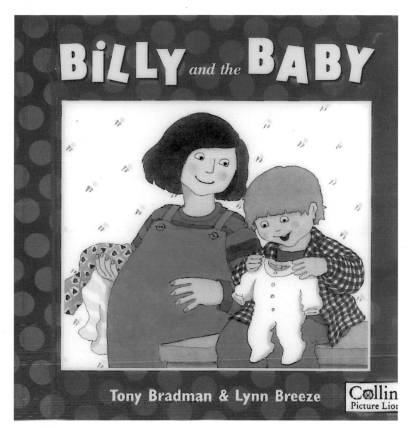

Published by Harper Collins Publishers Ltd.
ISBN: 0-00-664611-5
Illustrations © Lynn Breeze 1997

Billy and the Baby
Tony Bradman & Lynn Breeze

This story is a must for parents who worry about sibling jealousy. Everyone is so busy worrying about Billy that they fail to notice that he's not at all jealous at the prospect of having a new baby in the house and in fact is quite busy with a project of his own. He is making a very original present for his baby sister, which is quite handy at a later stage as well!

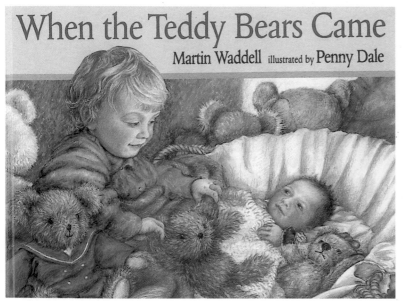

When the Teddy Bears Came
Martin Waddell illustrated by Penny Dale

Published by Walker Books Ltd.
ISBN: 0-7445-2569-1
Illustrations © Penny Dale 1994

## When the Teddy Bears Came
### Martin Waddell

When the new baby came to Tom's house so too did the teddy bears. Everyone brought a teddy for baby. Even Dad's long lost Bodger Bear reappeared. Mum has a great idea to make Tom feel useful. She needs help with all the teddies and then Mum, Dad and Tom all look after the baby. From initially feeling there was no room for him Tom finally becomes as indispensable as Mum and Dad in caring for the new baby. Warm family scenes are depicted on each page to further enhance the appeal of this book.

## Little Monster Did It!
### Helen Cooper

Little Monster and Amy's baby
brother come to live in Amy's
house at the same time.
Suddenly everything changes.
The peace and quiet in Amy's
house turns to mayhem. Is it
really Little Monster who is
causing trouble? Why does Amy
get the blame?
A great story to read aloud to
the little person in your house
whose space is invaded by a
baby brother or sister.

Published by Doubleday/Picture Corgi Books

ISBN: 0-552-52827-7

Illustrations © Helen Cooper 1995

## Daisy and the Egg
### Jane Simmons

Daisy is sent to visit and take food to Auntie Buttercup every day while she sits on her own eggs and on one for Daisy's Mum. However Daisy is adamant that she's not leaving her baby brother or sister to be, and decides to sit on the egg herself. Daisy is rewarded for her perseverance when her little brother Pip is born on a beautiful sunny morning. Text and illustration compliment each other ideally in this award winning picture book for two to five year olds.

Published by The O'Brien Press Ltd.
ISBN: 0-86278-624-X
Illustrations © Jane Simmons 1999

# Books to make you laugh

Published by Walker Books Ltd.
ISBN: 0-7445-5571-X
Illustrations © Jez Alborough 1998

## My Friend Bear
### Jez Alborough

A fun tale in rhyme that tells the further adventures of Eddy, Bear and their teddies. Children will love this larger than usual picture book with bright bold illustrations on double page spreads. As the story unfolds we see how Eddy and the bear become playmates with the help of their teddies.

## Isabel's Noisy Tummy
## David McKee

The subject of this hilarious book is Isabel's tummy. After days of rumbling in the classroom Isabel's tummy saves the day when the class visit the zoo. A loud roar frightens a ferocious tiger and makes Isabel a hero with her classmates. However, back in the classroom, all is quiet until Isabel's tummy rumbling is replaced by a different noise! Bold colourful illustrations and David McKee's wicked sense of humour make this an extremely enjoyable book.

Published by Andersen Press Ltd.
ISBN: 0-86264-497-6
Illustrations © David McKee 1994

## Goal!
### Colin McNaughton

A hilarious picture book, featuring the hero Preston Pig. Preston's mum asks him to go to the supermarket one day while he is playing football in the garden. Preston, the world's best footballer, sets off wreaking havoc on the way. As always he outwits his old enemy Mr Wolf who gets thrown out of the supermarket. Written in comic style this book will appeal to children aged five and up.

"A picture book of rare comic zest!"
Books for Keeps

Published by Andersen Press Ltd.
ISBN: 0-86264-727-4
Illustrations © Colin McNaughton 1997

Published by Andersen Press Ltd.

ISBN: 0-86264-581-6

Illustrations © Colin McNaughton 1996

## Oops!
Colin McNaughton

Winner of the 1996 Smarties Book Prize for under-fives. Another Preston Pig story to amuse young children. Preston re-enacts the Little Red Riding Hood story and tricks Mister Wolf yet again. Text and pictures are equally effective in making this another hilarious book for children.

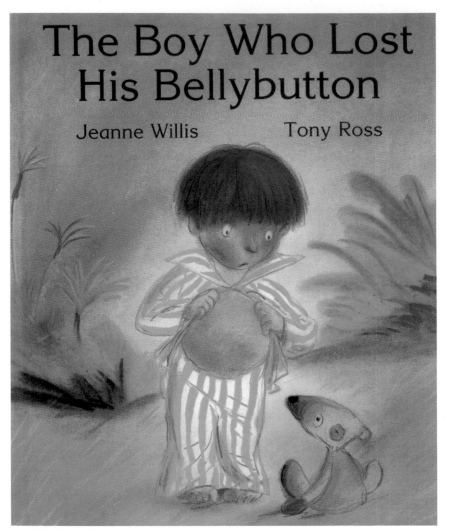

Published by Andersen Press Ltd.
ISBN: 0-86264-824-6
Illustrations © Tony Ross 1999

## The Boy Who Lost His Bellybutton
## Jeanne Willis & Tony Ross

The combination of words and illustrations from Jeanne Willis and Tony Ross produces a delightfully funny story. Just when you think the little boy is about to be eaten by the crocodile, he safely grabs back his missing bellybutton. A story that is sure to provide plenty of opportunity for discussion.

## Rover
## Michael Rosen

The idea of dogs being owned by humans is turned upside down in this story. Rover owns a pet human. A mixture of ordinary and comic style text works very well to give a hilarious view of us humans through the eyes of the ever sensible Rover.

Published by Bloomsbury Children's Books

ISBN: 0-7475-4020-9

Illustrations © Neal Layton 1999

# Stories that Rhyme

## Are You There, Baby Bear?
### Debi Gliori

Join Mr Bear in his search for Baby Bear through the woods where he meets lots of different animals and insects. Children will love this lift-the-flap novelty book, ideal for sharing and playing with. Mr Bear is made to appear foolish again as is the case in all the Mr Bear books by Debi Gliori. However things have a habit of sorting themselves out in the end for this endearing character that children love.

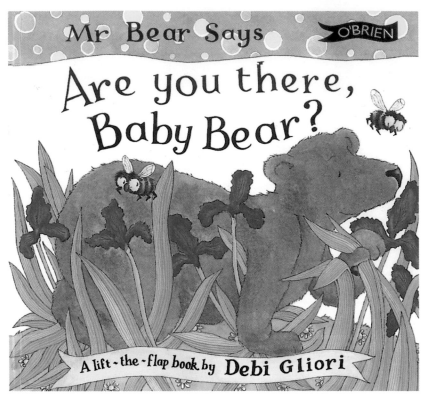

Published by The O'Brien Press Ltd.
ISBN: 0-86278-531-6
Illustrations © Debi Gliori 1997

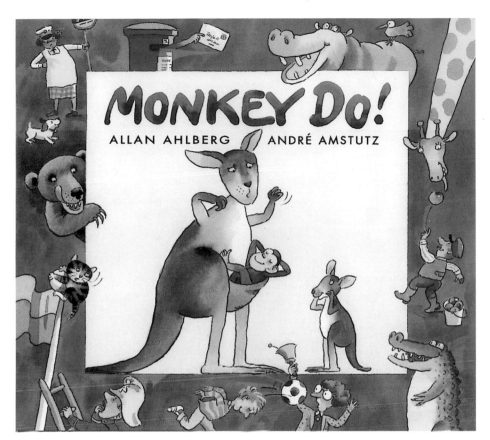

Published by Walker Books Ltd
ISBN: 0 7445-5573-6
Illustrations © André Amstutz 1998

## Monkey Do!
## Allan Ahlberg

Follow little monkey on his rampage out of the zoo and through the town. He has several narrow escapes before he returns to the safety of his mother late in the evening. Rhyming text in large print and bright lively pictures will have children reading this picture book over and over again.

# The Gruffalo
## Julia Donaldson

Published by Macmillan Children's Books
ISBN: 0-333-71093-2
Illustrations © Axel Scheffler 1999

A mouse's adventures in the deep dark wood is the subject of this picture book written in rhyming text. Young children between 3 and 6 will enjoy the story of this clever-thinking mouse and delight in the pictures on each page. The gruffalo who is described to be a fearsome monster in words is in fact cute and lovable in picture. Children will love this story and remember it long after it's been read.

*Ar fáil trí Ghaeilge dár dteideal,*

# This is the Bear
## Sarah Hayes

A simple story for small children, *This is the Bear* tells the story of a little boy's teddy who, with the help of the dog, ends up in the rubbish bin. What follows are the adventures of the teddy in amazingly few words. An adventure story with a happy ever after ending in large bold rhyming text and clear uncomplicated drawings combine to make this a lovely story for three to four year olds.

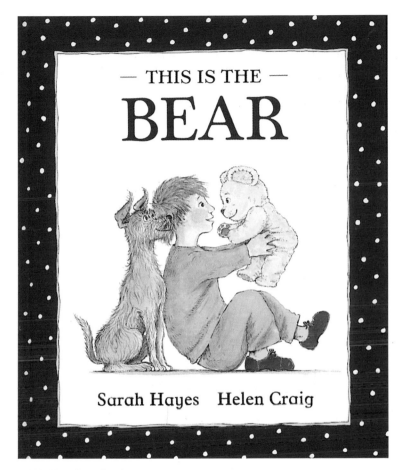

Published by Walker Books Ltd.
ISBN: 0-7445-1533-5
Illustrations © Helen Craig 1986

# Animals and Pets

## I Love Animals
### Flora McDonnell

Bright, bold drawings synonymous with Flora McDonnell make this a favourite with young children. A selection of farm animals takes up full double pages making it more a book for looking at and talking about rather than reading.

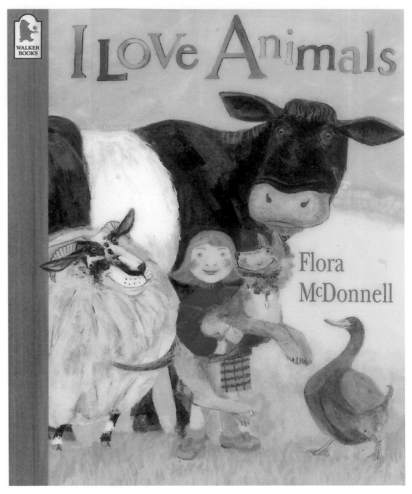

Published by Walker Books Ltd.

ISBN: 0-7445-4346-0

Illustrations © Flora McDonnell 1994

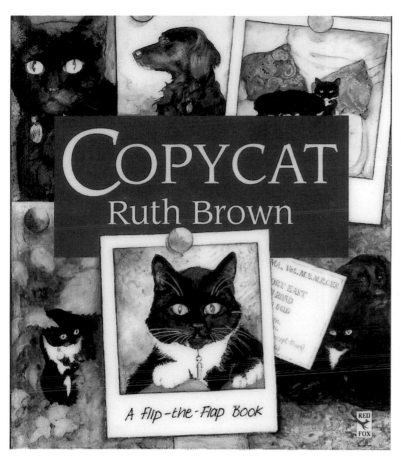

Published by Red Fox
ISBN: 0-09-960411-6
Illustrations © Ruth Brown 1994

## Copycat
## Ruth Brown

Buddy the copy cat goes too far with his copying one day and loses three teeth gnawing a bone like Bessie the dog. Even though his tongue hangs out a bit now, Buddy is not too worried. You can find out why on the last page of the book. This is a beautifully illustrated picture book, which will delight all cat lovers.

THERE'S A WARDROBE IN MY MONSTER!

Words by
Adrienne
Geoghegan

Pictures by
Adrian Johnson

Published by The Blackwater Press
ISBN: 0-7475-4109-5

Illustrations © Adrian Johnson 1999

## There's a Wardrobe in My Monster!
### Adrienne Geoghegan

Martha, bored with all the usual pets, decides she wants a monster for a pet. However she puts very little thought into what she will feed it. This monster eats everything wooden in sight. A funny tale with an underlying moral. Owning a pet can mean unforseen responsibilities.

## The Pig in the Pond
## Martin Waddell

When Neligan goes into town all the animals take the opportunity to enjoy themselves. The ducks and geese swim in the pond in the blazing sun while the pig looks on. She becomes more and more envious until she can't bear it anymore and she does something unheard of and jumps in. As if this isn't crazy enough she is joined by Neligan who also jumps in on his return from town. A combination of double page spreads and comic strip style illustrations enhances the fun in the story and makes it

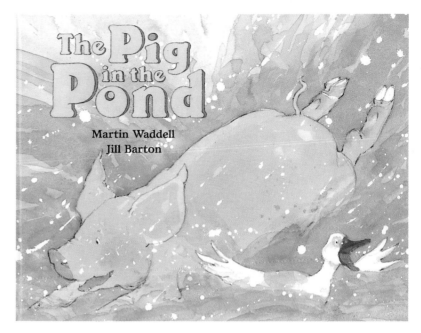

Published by Walker Books Ltd.
ISBN: 0-7445-2168-8
Illustrations © Jill Barton 1992

## The Great Pet Sale
### Mick Inkpen

Children will learn numbers, prices and the concept of having to pay for something in a shop by using this book, which is as much a toy as a book and is ideal for small children to explore. Rat tries hard to sell himself to the little boy in the story. Older children will be able to add the cost of the animals and will not be too surprised when the last page opens in a double spread to reveal that £1.00 is enough to buy Rat with half of his whiskers missing and all the other animals as well.

Published by Hodder Children's Books
ISBN: 0-340-72677-6
Illustrations © Mick Inkpen 1998

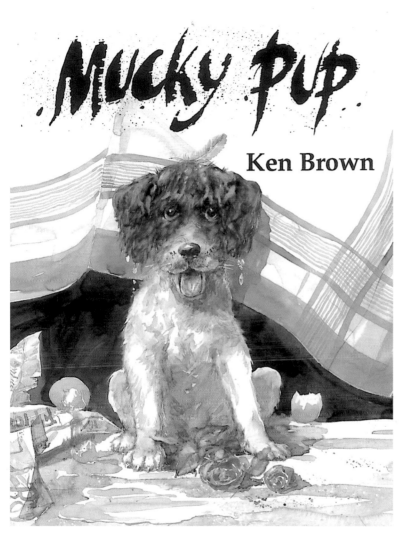

Published by Andersen Press Ltd.

ISBN: 0-86264-751-7

Illustrations © Ken Brown 1997

## Mucky Pup
### Ken Brown

The adorable illustrations of Mucky Pup are sure to endear all young readers to this mischievous little puppy that none of the other animals want to play with. None except a mucky pig that Mucky Pup plans to play with every day from now on. A suitable story for small children who like a happy ever after ending.

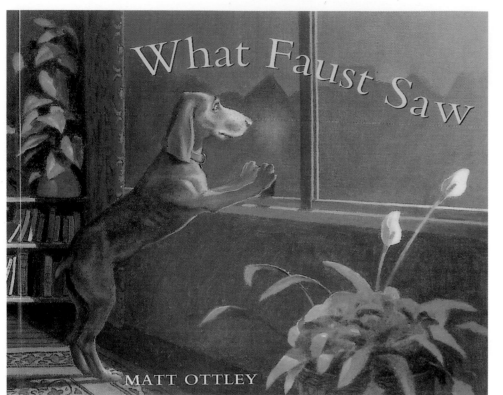

Published by Wolfhound Press
ISBN: 0-86327-603-2
Illustrations © Matthew Ottley 1995

## What Faust Saw
### Matt Ottley

Poor Faust has no one to comfort him when he sees something very strange in the night. The entire family reprimands him so much so that he decides to run away. After a night of adventures, mostly bad, he makes up his mind to go back to sleep next time he's awakened by anything strange.

## Just Like Floss
### Kim Lewis

The difficult choice of deciding which puppy to keep from the litter is solved in this book. Dad says we'll keep the puppy most like Floss to work on the farm and find good homes for all the others. Fantastic winter scenes and pictures of life on the farm make it a wonderful book for city and country children alike.

Published by Walker Books Ltd.
ISBN: 0-7445-6129-9
Illustrations © Kim Lewis 1998

Fantasy

# What If?
## Jonathan Shipton

A picture book sure to engage your child's imagination from the very start. Plenty of scope for discussion and an unusual opportunity to make up your own story at the end, something all children like to do. This is a great story for sharing.

Published by Macmillan Children's Books
ISBN: 0-333-73486-6
Illustrations © Barbara Nascimbeni 1999

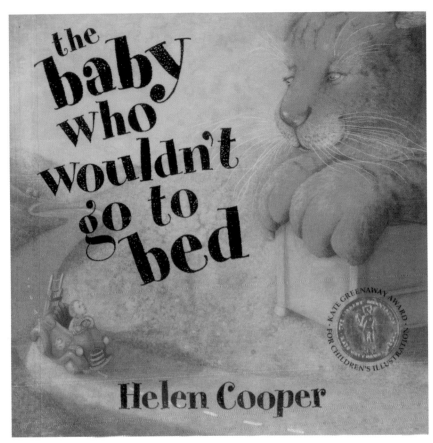

Published by Doubleday/Picture Corgi Books
ISBN: 0-552-52838-2
Illustrations © Helen Cooper 1996

## The Baby Who Wouldn't Go To Bed
### Helen Cooper

Winner of the Kate Greenaway Medal for illustration.
This story captures the imagination of a little boy who is determined not to go to sleep. The reader looks into the child's imagination and shares a magical adventure with him until his mother finds him and puts him to bed with a lot of love and affection. The pictures have everything it takes to make it a book of fantasy, humour and love, ideally suited to toddlers.

Published by Jonathan Cape Ltd.
ISBN: 0-224-02698-4
Illustrations © John Burningham 1989

## Oi! Get off our Train
### John Burningham

A little boy is ordered to go to sleep by his mum as she hands him his doggy pyjama-case for company. Playing with his toy train immediately before bed he continues his journey in his dreams. The little boy is asked by a selection of endangered animals if they can join him on his train. The book takes the child on an imaginary journey, amalgamating the world of play and fantasy with some rather serious issues.

*Ar fáil trí Ghaeilge dár dteideal Hé! Imigh leat den Traein.*

## Where the Wild Things Are
### Maurice Sendak

Having made mischief, Max is sent to bed early by his mother without his supper. It is that night that Max's great adventure begins. A forest grows with an ocean roaring by, on which Max sails on his private boat. Max tames all the wild things with their terrible roars. He becomes their king and has total control over them. However, even being king of the wild things has its drawbacks when a hungry child smells his supper and thinks about being where someone loves him best of all. Max returns to his own world after his great adventure.

**WHERE THE WILD THINGS ARE**

**STORY AND PICTURES BY MAURICE SENDAK**

Published by The Bodley Head Children's Books
ISBN: 0-370-00772-7
Illustrations © Maurice Sendak 1963

## It's a Jungle Out There
### Ed Miliano

Adults will enjoy this picture book just as much as children. An unusual jungle is explored by an unusual explorer. "Danger lurks everywhere, up high in the sky and down low on the ground," often unnoticed by us humans. The hero in this book is like us however, when he becomes hungry and exhausted after a hard day's work and needs to settle down for the night. A lovely story with striking illustrations to explore with children at bedtime.

It's A Jungle Out There

**Ed Miliano**

"Like all the great picture books, a delight for both adult and child."
Robert Dunbar, *lecturer and reviewer*

Published by Wolfhound Press
ISBN: 0-86327-570-2
Illustrations © Ed Miliano 1997

# Babysitters and Mums
# who go out to work

Published by Mammoth
ISBN: 0-7497-2749-7
Illustrations © Clara Vulliamy 1992

# Poor Monty
## Anne Fine

Monty's mother works as a doctor. After a tiring day on her rounds she fails to give Monty her full attention only to discover later in the evening that he has chicken pox. The situation is familiar to all working mothers who feel the need for just a few quiet moments on return from work. However once Mum turns her attention to Monty he begins to feel better already.

# When Mummy Comes Home Tonight
## Eileen Spinelli

For every working mother to share with her child. Striking illustrations in calm pastel shades echo the sense of intimacy and love between mother and child.

Published by Simon and Schuster UK Ltd.
ISBN: 0-689-82714-8
Illustrations © Jane Dyer 1998

## Mr Bear Babysits
### Debi Gliori

Mr Bear has to babysit the four young Grizzle-Bears, something which turns out to be a little more difficult than he thought. Children and adults will enjoy the observations of the young bears who say things like "You're not very good at that" when Mr Bear drenches himself while trying to bath the smallest Grizzle-Bear. A very funny story with amusing pictures combine to make this a favourite book.

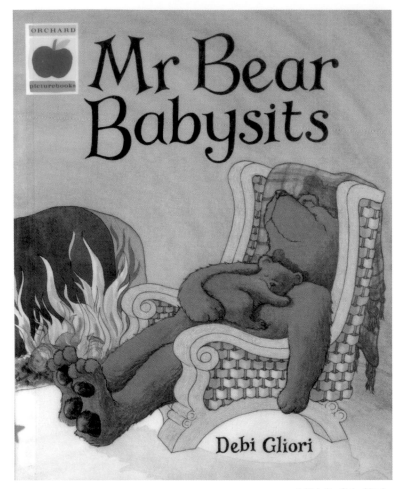

Published by Orchard Books
ISBN: 1-85213-843-2
Illustrations © Debi Gliori 1994

Published by Red Fox
ISBN: 0-09-925604-5
Illustrations © Shirley Hughes 1984

## An Evening at Alfie's
### Shirley Hughes

The ever popular picture book character, Alfie, is being looked after by his babysitter, Maureen. All is quiet to begin with but a burst pipe requires adult help. As with all Alfie stories a real situation is presented. Maureen, the reliable babysitter knows when she needs help and does everything to ensure the safety and happiness of Alfie and his baby sister Annie Rose. The interaction of illustration and text, both by Shirley Hughes, makes this a reassuring story that has long been a favourite.

When someone
you love dies

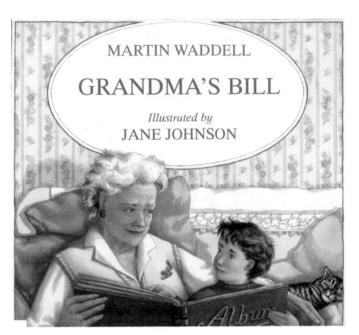

Published by Macdonald Young Books
ISBN: 0-7500-2627-8
Illustrations © Jane Johnson 1990

# Grandma's Bill
## Martin Waddell

"Who is this?"asks Bill, pointing to a photograph on his granny's mantlepiece. What follows is a moving evaluation of family life. Bill's granny compares her deceased husband, also named Bill, to her little grandson Bill at various stages of his development. The book takes us through the marriage of Bill's grandparents, their life together to old age and eventually to Grandfather's death. Little Bill looks for reassurance when he finds out his Grandda's dead. "It's alright, though, isn't it?" says Bill and Grandma replies, "of course it is."

# I'll Always Love You
## Hans Wilhelm

This is a beautiful book, which deals realistically and sensitively with the death of a little boy's best friend, his dog. The little boy's loss is made easier by his knowledge that he always loved his pet and always told him so. The pictures show the boy and Elfie the dog growing up together, learning and playing together in a real and imaginative way.

Published by Hodder Children's Books
ISBN: 0-340-40153-2
Illustrations © Hans Wilhelm, Inc. 1985

# All Shining in the Spring
## Siobhán Parkinson

Although this is not a picture book in the traditional format of the others in this collection, the story is ideal for an adult to read to a child who has experienced the death of a baby brother or sister. Simple words and drawings merge to produce a book that deals openly and sensitively with a painful subject. Siobhán Parkinson wrote this book for her son Matthew, then aged six, when she discovered her second child would die at birth. For any family who has experienced an infant death this book is an inspiration for adults and children alike.

Published by The O'Brien Press Ltd.
ISBN: 0-86278-387-9
Illustrations © The O'Brien Press Ltd. 1995

# Fears and Anxieties

Published by Walker Books Ltd.
ISBN: 0-7445-1316-2
Illustrations © Barbara Firth 1988

## Can't You Sleep, Little Bear?
### Martin Waddell

Like many small children Little Bear is afraid of the dark and can't sleep. But Big Bear is nearby to dispel his fears and provide him with light, first from lanterns in the cave and finally very cleverly from the moon. This is a reassuring story for any child who is afraid of the dark. An ideal story at bedtime.

*Ar fáil trí Ghaeilge dár dteideal* Oíche Mhaith a Bhéirín.

# Come On, Daisy!
## Jane Simmons

Daisy becomes so involved
in play that she doesn't
notice how far away from
Mama Duck she has
strayed. She chases
dragon flies, bounces on
the lilypads and plays with
a frog and only misses
Mama Duck when she
hears scary noises in the
reeds or high above her
head. Her safe familiar
pond only becomes
frightening when Mama
isn't there anymore.

Published by The O'Brien Press Ltd.
ISBN: 0-86278-552-9
Illustrations © Jane Simmons 199

## Just You and Me
### Sam McBratney

Little Goosey insists she wants to be on her own with Gander Goose when the storm comes. After exploring the homes of different woodland animals they settle in a hole behind a bush at the bottom of the hill. Even after the storm has passed and Little Goosey discovers the other animals shared their refuge while the great wind blew, she still stresses she wants "just you and me" to Gander Goose when a walk to the river is suggested.

Published by Walker Book's Ltd.
ISBN: 0-7445-5515-9
Illustrations © Ivan Bates 1998

# Traditional Tales
# with a difference

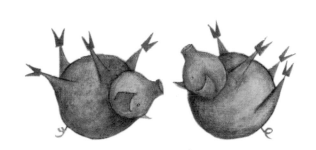

Published by Little Mammoth
ISBN: 0-7497-0024-6
Illustrations © Margaret Chamberlain 1988

## Look Out, He's Behind You!
### Tony Bradman
### & Margaret Chamberlain

A different twist to the traditional tale of Little Red Riding Hood and a lot less gory too. All the woodland animals help Little Red Riding Hood to make her journey safely to her granny's. A series of flaps on each page disclose the various hiding places of Mr. Wolf as he tries to sneak up on Little Red Riding Hood. Children will be delighted to see the Big Bad Wolf trapped in the woodcutter's shed when they lift the flap to open the door. This is an ideal book for adults and children to share and enjoy.

# Mrs. Goat and her Seven Little Kids
Tony Ross

The story and illustrations are hilarious in this book portraying a totally chaotic household consisting of Big Mother Goat and seven kids. No matter what the wolf does to impersonate Mother Goat the littlest kid is by far too smart for him. However, the other kids eventually open the door to the Hungry Wolf. But this is not the end. Read how Big Mother Goat gets back her six little kids, kisses them on the nose and slaps them on the ear for opening the door to a wolf.

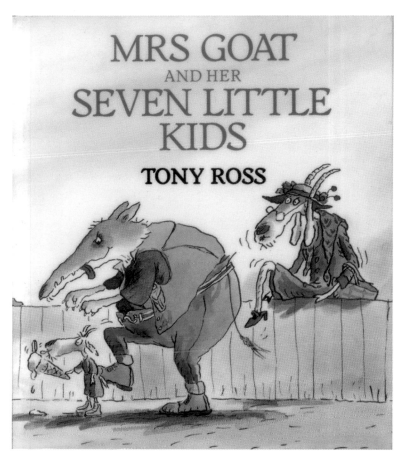

Published by Red Fox
ISBN: 0-09-976900-X
Illustrations © Tony Ross 1990

## The Gigantic Turnip
### Aleksei Tolstoy

Winner of the *Books for Children* Mother Goose Award.

Words and pictures go hand in hand to produce a stunning new version of this old tale. Children will enjoy the opportunity to join in and count as the story unfolds. After all the animals and the little old man and woman have exhausted themselves trying to pull the gigantic turnip, a surprise helper saves the day.

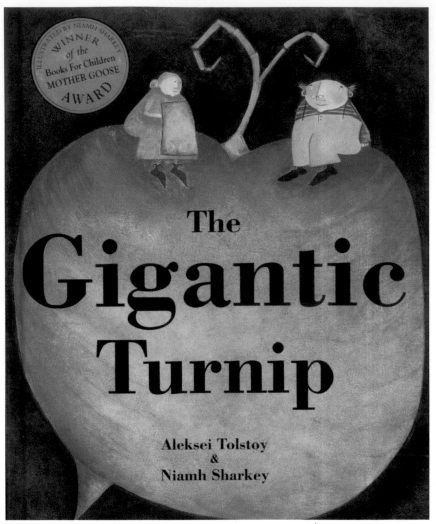

Published by Barefoot Books

ISBN: 0-902283-11-2

Illustrations © Niamh Sharkey 1998

Published by Walker Books Ltd.

ISBN: 0-7445-6124-8

Illustrations © Helen Oxenbury 1999

## Alice's Adventures in Wonderland
## Helen Oxenbury

A renowned illustrator, Helen Oxenbury has won several awards for her work. Her treatment of this classic story by Lewis Carroll is guaranteed to delight and inspire children of the new millennium to read it. The pictures on every double page make the story more tangible and accessible than ever before. The Alice in this story is a character that today's child can relate to. Once given this book the reader will want to keep it forever.

Published by Puffin Books
ISBN: 0-14-054056-3
Illustrations © Lane Smith 1989

# The True Story of the Three Little Pigs by A. Wolf
## Jon Scieszka

A hilarious retelling of the traditional story. If you thought you knew the story of the three little pigs, think again. Here is Mr Wolf's version of events. He tells of how he sets out to make a birthday cake for his granny and ends up being framed and sent to prison. Suitable for somewhat older children, who need to be able to understand the parody and wit which make the story so funny.

# Stories to Share
## at Bedtime

## Bunny My Honey
### Anita Jeram

Mummy Rabbit teaches her little bunny all the "rabbity" things he needs to know. Life is ideal in the woods for Bunny and his friends until one day Bunny gets lost. But just as Mummy was always there to comfort her Little Bunny, she is here now too to reassure him and tell him she loves him when she finds him. A gentle reassuring story for all little children who, just like Bunny, need Mummy's supervision and love to feel safe and happy.

Published by Walker Books Ltd.
ISBN: 0-7445-6162-0
Illustrations © Anita Jeram 1999

Published by Bloomsbury Children's Books
ISBN: 0-7475-4110-8
Illustrations © Debi Gliori 1999

## No Matter What
## Debi Gliori

"I'm a grim and grumpy little Small and nobody loves me at all," said a small fox. These words are familiar to all parents who undoubtedly are approached by their own little "Smalls" at some time when they seek reassurance of love and affection. Rhyming text and fantastic illustrations make this an award-winning picture book to treasure. Serious questions are asked and answered in the subtlest way, for instance in the closing lines of the book. As Large and Small look out at the night we read "Still they shine in the evening skies - love - like starlight, never dies."

## Cuddly Dudley
### Jez Alborough

A lovely book to snuggle up with at bedtime, Cuddly Dudley tells the story of a cuddly penguin who just wants to be left alone for a while. The pictures tell the story so there is very little need for words, which is probably why they are kept to a minimum in this delightful picture book.

Published by Walker Books Ltd.
ISBN: 0-7445-3607-3
Illustrations © Jez Alborough 1993

## Tell Me Something Happy Before I Go To Sleep
### Joyce Dunbar & Debi Gliori

A perfect book for bedtime and especially for little people who think they might not be able to go to sleep. When Willa can't sleep, her loving brother Willoughby suggests she think of all the happy things she will wake up to in the morning. Willa drifts off to sleep in the reassuring knowledge that best of all her brother will also be there when she wakes up next morning. Warm bedtime scenes excellently illustrated by Debi Gliori add to the beauty of the story.

Published by Doubleday
ISBN: 0-385-40791-2
Illustrations © Debi Gliori 1998

## Guess How Much I Love You
### Sam McBratney

Telling someone how much you love them is the subject of this book. Big and Little Nutbrown Hare try to measure how much they love each other in relation to the world they live in, a difficult thing to do. The love between father and son is explored here. By writing about Daddy Hare and his little son, the world of animals is used to enable the young child to compare and explore these emotions in relation to him or herself. A beautiful book for parent and child to share.

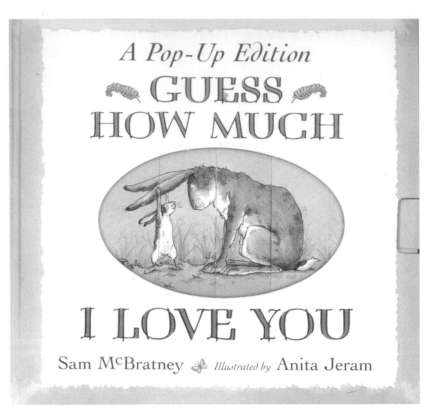

Published by Walker Books Ltd.
ISBN: 0-7445-6180-9
Illustrations © Anita Jeram 1994, 1998

Published by Walker Books Ltd.
ISBN: 0-7445-2166-1
Illustrations © Patrick Benson 1992

## Owl Babies
## Martin Waddell

Three little owls wake up one night to find that Owl Mother has gone. They experience the very real stages of anxiety that any little children might go through on finding they are left alone. As in many picture books the fears and anxieties of the child are explored through animals, in this case the owlets, Sarah, Percy and Bill. One can't help but smile at the little owls when mother asks what all the fuss is about on her return. Safe in their mother's presence they each declare "I knew it", when mother says "You knew I'd come back."

# Leabhair Gaeilge

**MAMÓ AG AN ZÚ**
MARY ARRIGAN

**LÁ le MAMÓ**
MARY ARRIGAN

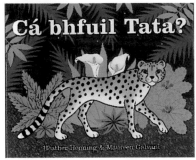

**Cá bhfuil Tata?**
Heather Henning & Maureen Galvani

**MAMÓ AR AN FHEIRM**
MARY ARRIGAN

AN GÚM

**MAMÓ COIS TRÁ**
MARY ARRIGAN

Tá méadú ag teacht ar an méid leabhair Ghaeilge le pictiúir atá ar fáil i gcónaí. Tá cuid de na leabhair ar a rinne léirmheas orthu i mBéarla ar fáil trí Ghaeilge freisin. Tá leabhair oiriúnacha ar fáil faoin gcuid is mó de na teidil thuas, is cuma an leabhar atá uait chun uimhreacha, cruthanna, nó méid a mhíniú nó díreach gur mhaith leat scéal maith a roinnt le do pháiste.

Seo a leanas cuid de na leabhair le pictiúir trí Ghaeilge atá molta:
*Lá le Mamó* le Mary Arrigan
*Léigh Mamó ar an Fheirm*, *Mamó cois Trá*, *Mamó ag an Zú*, leis an údar céanna.

*Cití Cailleach* agus *Cití sa Gheimhreadh* le Korky Paul agus Valerie Thomas
*Cá bhfuil Tata* le Heather Henning

*Cruthanna*
*Dathanna*
*Céard é féin?*
*An Fheirm*
*An Teach*

Tá siad seo go léir foilsithe ag An Gúm

Tá na leabhair Spot le Eric Hill ar fáil trí Ghaeilge freisin ach go dtugtar Bran ar an laoch sa leagan Gaeilge! Bainfidh páistí an-taitneamh as eachtraí Bhrain agus é ag ceiliúradh a lá breithe, a chéad lá ar scoil agus ullmhúchain na Nollag.

I measc na dteideal tá:
*Bran agus an Nollaig*
*Léann Bran an tAm*
*Bran ag an Sorcas*
*Bran agus a chairde ag Súgradh.*